AbzuGLUTely!
BATTLING, BELLOWING
BELLA ABZUG

Illustrated by

SARAH ARONSON

ANDREA D'AQUINO

CALKINS CREEK
AN IMPRINT OF ASTRA BOOKS FOR YOUNG READERS
New York

"I wanted to be a lawyer ever since I was a little kid. I had no role models. But I always thought if I could become a lawyer I COULD SET THINGS STRAIGHT."

Bella Savitzky Abzug was never a sugar-and-spice gal.

Growing up in the Bronx in the 1920s, Bella enjoyed trading baseball cards, playing checkers and marbles, and riding her bike. She was fiercely competitive—a whiz kid with a wild streak—and the streets were her playground. She drew graffiti with her friends all over New York City.

Her parents trusted her. They were hardworking
Jewish immigrants who fled wartime Russia in search of
religious freedom and a chance to make a better life.

They raised their daughters with music and prayer and a
strict moral code founded in Judaism. Charity was important,
but it was just a first step. In Bella's family, *tikkun
olam* (repairing of the world) meant justice.
Not just for themselves. But for everyone else, too.

Her parents were no strangers to protest. To broadcast their desire for peace, they named their butcher shop the Live and Let Live Meat Market. This did not boost business.

But Bella got their message loud and clear! To make a difference in this world, you have to be bold. And brazen. And true to your heart.

And above all, you can't be afraid to speak your truth.

By age eleven, Bella knew in her heart she wanted to be a lawyer and activist. For practice, she preached in the subway. She and her friends held out coffee cans to raise money for Zionist causes and organizations— for Jews to have a homeland.

It was in synagogue where Bella experienced injustice firsthand—and had to do something about it. Although she loved learning Talmud and singing the prayers, Bella resented having to stand in the back with the women and girls.

When her father died, enough was enough. Thirteen-year-old Bella mourned for her father the way only men were allowed to do, by chanting Kaddish, a prayer for the dead, every day for a year. In the front.

Day after day, nobody said anything. Maybe, like Bella, they didn't think those rules were fair. Maybe they felt sorry for her. Or maybe they could already see that there was no point trying to stop her.

This girl was born bellowing.
The world better watch out!

At Hunter College, Bella used her power as student council president to lead an all-women model Congress and attend lobbying trips to Washington, DC. She organized large rallies for free education and against the war raging overseas. And when she fell in love with Martin Abzug, she told him as clearly as possible: Her career would be just as important as his.

Without hesitation, Martin promised to support her ambition. And help raise their children. He even promised to do all her typing—since she never bothered to learn. This unconventional dream team were already married in 1945, when Bella—fresh out of Columbia Law School—began putting her beliefs (and her voice) to the test.

In the courtroom, Bella had a fierce moral compass.
She was never intimidated by tough cases or bullies, even
when her safety was threatened (which it was—a few times).
In the 1950s, she was one of the few lawyers who stood up
for the celebrities wrongly accused of being un-American
Communists by the biggest, most powerful bully of her
time—Senator Joseph McCarthy from Wisconsin.

On the streets, Bella joined forces with friends and leading feminists like Gloria Steinem and Betty Friedan. Together, they teamed up with 50,000 women in sixty cities around the United States to demonstrate against the Vietnam War and nuclear arms. When Bella bellowed, "All issues are women's issues," people cheered.

ALL ISSUES are WOMEN'S ISSUES!

They knew she was talking about everything from racial and social justice to equal wages, childcare, peace, and protecting the environment.

To put it politely, Bella was a trailblazer. A serious woman. Ahead of her time.

To put it not so politely, this passionate perfectionist was demanding and loud. A radical contrarian. Too ambitious to work with.

For all of those reasons, New Yorkers adored her.
They couldn't get enough of her homegrown CHUTZPAH,
her low gravelly voice, and especially her trademark
wide-brimmed hats.
She wore them everywhere.
They were never a fashion statement.

Bella wore hats because she *had* to wear hats, because those wide-brimmed beauties represented authority and power, the very things she was still battling for in 1970, when at the age of fifty, she wondered if maybe she might get more done from the inside—rather than out.

That meant: a run for Congress.

It didn't take her long to find the perfect battle cry. A worn-out adage, turned upside-down.

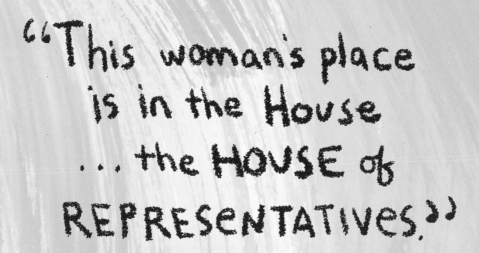

"This woman's place is in the House ... the HOUSE of REPRESENTATIVES."

And she WON!

Bella Abzug was the second Jewish woman ever elected to Congress. She was also the first woman elected to Congress on a women's rights platform. After taking the official oath of office on January 3, 1971, Bella marched outside to the House steps and took a "people's oath" administered by the first Black woman elected to Congress, her colleague Congresswoman Shirley Chisholm.

Onlookers cheered, " Give 'em hella, BELLA!"

(Honestly, she didn't need any encouragement.)

For the next six years, Battling Bella brought the voice of protest to politics. She bellowed for the ideals that mattered to women.

She sponsored bills dedicated to justice, from women's equality, civil rights, disability rights, to equal pay.

She was a prominent voice against the Vietnam War. She was the first congressperson to introduce a national gay rights bill.

No surprise, the backlash was brutal.
Her colleagues called her polarizing.
Shrill. They implied that working with
her cost *them* too many votes.
    If it bothered her,
it didn't stop her.

By 1976, *U.S. News & World Report*
considered Bella the third most influential
person in Congress. She had graced the
cover of *Life* magazine and signed
autographs everywhere she went.

But instead of running for reelection, Bella
set her sights on a bigger arena—the United States
Senate. Unfortunately, voters weren't quite ready
for Senator Abzug. Later, when she ran for mayor
of New York City, she lost that race, too.

Without an office, Battling Bella could have slowed down. But her truth hadn't changed. There was still work to do. Barriers to break down. People to fight for.

She predicted,

"Women will run the 21st century...and young people are going to be its leaders."

This was her hope and her dream. The future she fought for.

With her big, brazen voice, Battling Bella Abzug did much more than bellow. This pioneer wrote a whole new playbook for women in politics and across the nation. She didn't get everything she fought for, but she got the battle started.
So your voices could be heard.
And you could keep battling.
With a hat. Or without.

AUTHOR'S NOTE

In 1971, the year Bella Abzug took the people's pledge, I was a nine-year-old Jewish girl living in Bethlehem, Pennsylvania (also known as the Christmas City). At that time, many girls I knew were encouraged to be polite. And not interrupt. Loud meant unlikable.

That was particularly tough on me, since I already had a penchant for speaking my mind. (I could be pretty dramatic.) An older cousin fostered my interest in feminism and politics. It's no surprise to me that almost immediately, I became interested and excited by the work and voice of Bella Abzug.

She had a gigantic personality. Flair like a celebrity. She had a strong New York accent—just like my dad.

Best of all, she was Jewish. And outspoken. Like me.

Now we recognize how powerful it is for kids to see themselves in story. I can attest that it was amazing to see a Jewish woman holding power, speaking loudly—raising a ruckus—saying what she believed. Her bravery made me brave. Her passion made me want to march for women's rights (and a whole bunch of other things), too. It's one of the reasons this book is so important to me.

What I think you should know about Bella: She was ahead of her time, and she got no props for that, but that didn't stop her. Take any movement—she was there before it was popular. Bella Abzug was guided by a moral, ethical need to set the world on a course that was fair. And just. And equitable. And she never slowed down! Biographer and scholar, Leandra Zarnow wrote that Bella "lived out the maxim *lo dayenu*—it is not good enough, and we will not be satisfied."

Many of the things we are fighting for now, she fought for then.

Here's a short list: Bella Abzug fought for civil rights, women's rights, disability rights, and LGBTQ rights. She supported the Freedom of Information Act, the Equal Credit Opportunity Act, and Title IX. She fought for mass transportation and environmental protections. She battled for equal wages and child care and even universal health care. Her first vote in the House was for the Equal Rights Amendment. I think this is interesting:

Bella Abzug campaigns for Congress in 1970.

Bella Abzug was an idealist, but she believed in debate. Disagreement didn't intimidate her. Her blunt style was not always appreciated, but she inspired great loyalty from her friends and allies. For example: President Jimmy Carter named her chair of the National Advisory Committee for Women. When he dismissed her, twenty-three women on the committee went with her.

She never slowed down.

Without an office or voters to please, Bella traveled the world, made as many speeches as she wanted, wrote books, and organized conferences to support women in leadership. As the news media expanded, she found new ways to talk directly to Americans—on CNN. Behind the scenes, she put pressure on the Democratic leadership to add a woman to the presidential ticket. Nothing else would do!

And in 1984, Democratic presidential nominee Walter Mondale listened. Geraldine Ferraro took the stage as the nominee for vice president.

Bella reflected, "They used to give us a day—it was called International Women's Day. In 1975 they gave us a year, the Year of the Woman. Then from 1975 to 1985 they gave us a decade, the Decade of the Woman. I said at the time, who knows, if we behave they may let us into the whole thing. Well, we didn't behave and here we are."

And she was right!

Today, Bella Abzug's legacy is proof that your voice matters—that if you know something that will make the world better, you should go ahead and say it. Get to work! Empathy is not complete without action.

Let's take it from Bella: a woman's place *is* in the House. And the Senate. And the Supreme Court. In 2020, we elected Vice President Kamala Harris.

Bella's life shows us that when women work together, there is nothing we can't do.

Back in 1971, Bella Abzug made me want to vote. She also made me want to march and write letters. Today, she still makes me want to bellow about all the things that are important to me. Bellowing is a good thing.

As she would tell you, "It's what's under the hat that counts."

The last mile of the torch relay from Seneca Falls, NY, to Houston, TX, for the opening of the first National Women's Conference in 1977. From left to right: unknown, Billie Jean King, Susan B. Anthony II, Bella Abzug, Sylvia Ortiz, Peggy Kokernot, Michelle Cearcy, and Betty Friedan.

BELLA'S WORLD

1902: Manny Savitzky leaves Russia for America. His future wife Esther Tanklefsky arrives in 1907.

November 7, 1916: Jeannette Rankin, of Montana, is the first woman to be elected to the U.S. House of Representatives.

July 24, 1920: Bella is born in the Bronx, New York.

August 18, 1920: The Nineteenth Amendment to the Constitution is ratified, ensuring the right of women to vote.

January 12, 1932: Hattie Wyatt Caraway, of Arkansas, becomes the first woman elected to the U.S. Senate when her husband dies in office. She is reelected two times.

1939–1945: World War II

1944: Bella marries Martin Abzug.

1945: Bella graduates from Columbia Law School, where she is an editor of the *Columbia Law Review*. In 1945, Bella begins twenty-five years of practicing law.

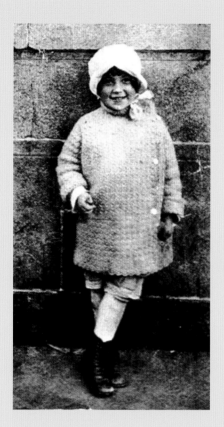

Bella Abzug at five years old

1949: Daughter Eve is born.

1950s: Bella focuses on civil rights and labor law. She boldly defends several actors before Senator Joseph McCarthy's House Un-American Activities Committee and its counterpart in Albany, New York. Later, she would say, "the Constitution permits any kind of ideas and thinking you please to have, and that no government has a right to interfere, ask questions, or challenge that thinking."

1952: Daughter Liz is born.

1954–75: Vietnam War

1961: Bella joins and helps grow the nationwide organization Women Strike for Peace.

June 10, 1963: The Equal Pay Act is passed by Congress, promising equitable wages for the same work, regardless of the race, color, religion, national origin, or sex of the worker.

1970: Bella wins election to Congress representing Manhattan's 19th Congressional District. During her campaign, stars stage *Broadway for Bella* at Madison Square Garden. Actress Barbra Streisand hosts a fundraiser for Bella on a flatbed truck.

August 26, 1970: More than 50,000 women marched down Fifth Avenue to celebrate the fiftieth anniversary of suffrage.

1971: Bella cofounds the National Women's Political Caucus with Shirley Chisolm, Patsy Takemoto Mink, Betty Friedan, and others.

1978: Appointed cochair of President Carter's National Advisory Committee for Women; fired in 1979 for criticizing the administration.

June 30, 1982: The Equal Rights Amendment, a very simple amendment putting protection for women directly into the United States Constitution, falls three states short of the thirty-eight states needed for ratification.

Bella Abzug (left) raises her hand as she is sworn in by Carl Albert (center) and Hale Boggs (right) during the opening session of the 92nd Congress, Washington, DC, January 1971.

July 12, 1984: Geraldine Ferraro becomes the first woman to be nominated as vice president on a major party ticket.

1991: With Mim Kelber, Bella cofounds the international Women's Environment and Development Organization (WEDO).

1994: Bella is inducted into the National Women's Hall of Fame in Seneca Falls, New York.

1998: Bella Abzug dies of complications following heart surgery in New York City on March 31 at age seventy-seven. At her funeral, First Lady Hillary Rodham Clinton and others pay tribute to Bella. The UN tribute to Bella is led by Secretary-General Kofi Annan.

Jan. 4, 2007: U.S. Representative Nancy Pelosi (D-Calif.) becomes the first female Speaker of the House. In 2019, she reclaims the title, becoming the first lawmaker to hold the office two times in more than fifty years.

June 7, 2016: Hillary Rodham Clinton secures the Democratic presidential nomination, becoming the first U.S. woman to lead the ticket of a major party.

2017: Congress has a record number of women, with 104 female House members and 21 female senators, including the chamber's first Latina, Nevada senator Catherine Cortez Masto.

January 20, 2021: Kamala Harris is sworn in as the first woman and first woman of color vice president of the United States. "While I may be the first woman in this office, I will not be the last," Harris said after getting elected in November.

BIBLIOGRAPHY

Abzug, Bella. *Bella!: Ms. Abzug Goes to Washington.* New York: Saturday Review Press, 1972.

Abzug, Bella and Mim Kelber. *Gender Gap: Bella Abzug's Guide to Political Power for American Women.* Boston: Houghton Mifflin, 1984.

"Abzug, Bella Savitzky." Biographical Directory of the United States Congress. bioguide.congress.gov/search/bio/a000018.

"Bella Abzug." Jewish Women's Archive. jwa.org/womenofvalor/abzug.

"Bella Abzug Biography." Biography.com. A&E Television Networks, May 12, 2021. biography.com/people/bella-abzug-9174815.

"Bella Abzug Biography." Encyclopedia of World Biography. notablebiographies.com/A-An/Abzug-Bella.html.

Cook, Blanche Wiesen, "Bella Abzug." *Jewish Women: A Comprehensive Historical Encyclopedia*. Jewish Women's Archive, 31 December 1999. jwa.org/encyclopedia/article/abzug-bella.

Faber, Doris. *Bella Abzug.* New York: Lothrop, Lee & Shepard Company, 1976.

Freeman, Jo. "Review of *Bella Abzug: How One Tough Broad from the Bronx Fought Jim Crow and Joe McCarthy, Pissed Off Jimmy Carter, Battled for the Rights of Women and Workers, Rallied Against War and for the Planet, and Shook Up Politics Along the Way.*" jofreeman.com/reviews/abzug.html.

Levine, Suzanne Braun, and Mary Thom. *Bella Abzug: How One Tough Broad from the Bronx Fought Jim Crow and Joe McCarthy, Pissed Off Jimmy Carter, Battled for the Rights of Women and Workers, Rallied Against War and for the Planet, and Shook Up Politics Along the Way.* New York: Farrar, Straus & Giroux, 2008.

MacPherson, Myra. "Bella Abzug, Champion of Women." *Washington Post,* April 2, 1988.

Mark, Jonathan, Steve Lipman, and James D. Besser. "Bella Abzug's Jewish Heart." *The New York Jewish Week*, April 3, 1998.

Office of the Historian. "Abzug, Bella Savitzky." History, Art & Archives, United States House of Representatives. history.house.gov/People/Detail/8276#biography.

"Personality: Bellacose Abzug." *Time*, August 16, 1971. content.time.com/time/subscriber/article/0,33009,877192-2,00.html.

Steinem, Gloria. *My Life on the Road.* New York: Random House, 2016.

Steinhauer, Jennifer. *The Firsts: The Inside Story of the Women Reshaping Congress.* New York: Algonquin Books, 2021.

Zarnow, Leandra Ruth. *Battling Bella: The Protest Politics of Bella Abzug.* Cambridge, MA: Harvard University Press, 2019.

Bella in the 1980s

ACKNOWLEDGMENTS

It's been my privilege and honor to write about the life of Bella Abzug—and it's been fun, too! Along the way, I relied on the support, instincts, intelligence and enthusiasm of many strong women. I offer my gratitude to them here.

Huge thanks to my editor, Carolyn Yoder, for her patience and tenacity. To Tanya Lee Stone, Melanie Fishbane, Carolyn Crimi, Laura Ruby, Jenny Meyerhoff, Brenda Ferber, Sarah Davies, and the writing community at the Highlights Foundation for their enthusiasm and endless support. I am especially indebted to Liz Abzug and historians Leandra Zarnow and Cynthia Harrison for their time, expert knowledge, and reviews, as well as Diana Mara Henry, the Jewish Women's Archive and Columbia University Library. And last, to my family for listening to all my stories, discoveries, and process. It can't be easy to raise a loud girl with so much to say. Your love has made me fearless.

PICTURE CREDITS

For Tanya Lee Stone and all the trailblazers of tomorrow —*SA*

For my grandmother, Teresa Galeano, who raised her family in the Bronx. She was a feminist well before that term was widely known or used. —*AD*

Calkins Creek
An imprint of Astra Books for Young Readers,
a division of Astra Publishing House
astrapublishinghouse.com

Printed in China

ISBN: 978-1-63592-807-5 (hc)
ISBN: 978-1-63592-808-2 (eBook)
Library of Congress Control Number: 2023914235

First edition

10 9 8 7 6 5 4 3 2 1

Design by Barbara Grzeslo
The text is set in Calibri.
The illustrations are done in colored inks, colored pencils, and wax crayon.
Illustrations published by arrangement with Debbie Bibo Agency.